CONTENTS

Welcome to the Legenderry City!

Céad míle fáilte to the greatest little city in the world!

If this is your first time visiting Derry, a word to the wise – pace yourself. There is so much to see and to do, you will be punctured by the time you leave. (Health warning: don't try to keep up with the locals.)

This is a city that is ancient but young, active yet tranquil, cultured and cutting edge. It is metropolitan and rural - and sits on the doorstep of the finest beaches in Ireland. Whether you're here for an overnight or a month, you're going to end up wishingtt you lived here.

Every visitor's need is catered for, from 6th-century pilgrim walks to 21st-century Derry Girls tours. Historians, sports fans, politics nuts, shoppers, music lovers and culture vultures - young or old - it matters not. You will find your bliss here.

Arrive any time, there'll be lots to do. There's jazz and choral festivals in the spring; sport, sea and sand in the summer; drama and Halloween hijinks in the autumn; rounded off with weeks of Christmas markets and magic - this really is the city that never sleeps.
From one end of the year to the next, our many entertainment venues feature non-stop programmes of music, film, theatre and art - all demonstrating why Derry was so deserving of its Capital of Culture title in 2013.

This is also a city of 'legend-Derry' hospitality, full of high-end restaurants, old world cafés, trad bars, rock pubs and techno venues. And if you can get better value anywhere on these islands - hats off to you.

This summer, a hotel room for two adults in Derry will cost 40 percent less than you'd pay in Belfast, and less than half of what you'd pay in Dublin* – and most deals here come with free parking and breakfast. [*The average price for a room in one of the top ten best (TripAdvisor) deals in Derry for the night of June 30, 2023 was £124.10, against £207.80 (Belfast) and £275.30 (Dublin - sterling), as booked on March 20, 2023.]

And shoppers, get out those cards! Derry is currently the only major city on the island of Ireland - or, indeed, in Europe - with immediate, unfettered access to both the EU and the UK - a trader's paradise. If we haven't got your bargain in the city, our Donegal neighbours just down the road will be all too happy to help.

So, enjoy your stay, tell all your friends and then start planning your next trip here.

Slán tamall and see you soon!

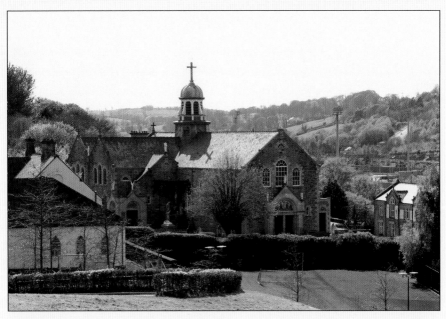

St Columba's Church (Long Tower),

Tower Museum

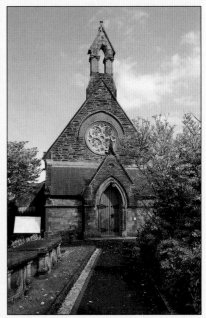

St Augustine's

ANCIENT GROUND
NEOLITHIC DERRY

Archaeologists tell us that Derry has been inhabited for at least 6,000 years.

Two recent digs, at Thornhill on the west bank of the River Foyle (2000) and Clooney Road on the east bank (2020), uncovered neolithic settlements.

The latter find, which featured recently on BBC TV's 'Digging for Britain', included two large rectangular buildings along with tools, pottery and cooking utensils.

At Thornhill, a palisaded enclosure said to have been home to 50 people was unearthed, suggesting evidence of Ireland's first settled farming community. Artefacts from this dig are on show at the award-winning Tower Museum.

In 2018, a hoard of gold bracelets believed to be from a Bronze Age (1200 to 800BC) trading post, was found at Tullydonnell, County Donegal, 15 miles southwest of Derry. This find is now on display at the National Museum of Ireland in Dublin, as is the Broighter Hoard of gold ornaments dating from the 1st century BC, found outside Limavady, 15 miles north of Derry, in the 1890s.

EARLY CHRISTIAN ERA

Three miles from Derry lies Grianán of Aileach, a restored hilltop stone fort dating back to early Christian times. It affords stunning views of Donegal, Derry and, on a clear day, Scotland. St Patrick's Holy Well, said to have healing powers and which was blessed by our patron saint, is found 100 yards from the fort. (Old joke: if you can see Errigal from Grianán, it means it's going to rain...if you can't see it, it's already raining.)

St Augustine's Church on Derry's ancient walls is said to have been the site of Derry's first Christian settlement, the Dubh Regles monastery, built in the mid-6th century on an oakgrove (Doire) by the city's founder Colmcille. Enjoying the magnificent view of the new city from this vantage point, it is possible to pick out the Long Tower Church (1784, remodelled 1908), named after the 12th century bell tower, the Túr Fada, once the tallest building in Ireland.

The exact site of the original tower is still under dispute. Most archaeologists and historians assert it is in fact the Siege Windmill still standing on the grounds of Lumen Christi College, as carbon dating shows the mortar in the tower to be from the 12th century. Others such as Derry's Streets historian, John Bryson, locate the Túr Fada within the grounds of the Long Tower a few hundred yards away and argue that the windmill was built from debris following the demolition of the tower.

The Áras Cholmcille Centre in the grounds of the Long Tower contains a small museum examining the area's ancient (and modern) history.

Derry's Túr Fada

MEDIEVAL TIMES

During the middle ages (1150s), an Augustinian monastery, An Teampall Mór, was built in Derry [Bryson puts it contiguous to the Siege Windmill and the Long Tower church, others put it closer to the site of St Columb's Cathedral]. A Dominican Convent was erected in the Bogside in the late 13th century (1270s) close to where St Eugene's Cathedral (1863) was later located.

Grianán Fort

A pilgrim trail, Túras Cholmcille, which attracted thousands of visitors to Daire, ran from the Foyle through the Bogside and past the holy St Columb's Wells, around the belltower and uphill to the Dubh Regles. The trail was reenacted in 2013 for Derry's City of Culture celebrations.

Of the three original wells, only the one to Colmcille is still operational, functioning as the centrepoint of Derry's annual Columban celebrations on June 9.

The starting point for the trail was Tower House, home of the O'Doherty clan, which would have been at the bank of the river when it was built in the early 1500s, and is now the site of the Tower Museum at Union Hall Place.

The museum chronicles the region's history from Neolithic times right up to the recent Troubles, and includes an exhibition on a number of ships from the Spanish Armada which sank off Donegal and were subsequently excavated.

Across the Peace Bridge on the east bank of the Foyle (a.k.a. The Waterside), the remains of the late-16th century St Brecan's Church can be found in St Columb's Park. The church was built in 1585 by Bishop Redmond O'Gallagher on the site of an earlier mediaeval church destroyed in 1197. In 1601, O'Gallagher was killed, along with 80 civilians, by soldiers under the command of the English general Sir Henry Docwra during the conquest of Ulster.

9

Early photograph of Carlisle Bridge, c. 1865

The Courthouse and Bishop's Place on Bishop Street, c 1860s.

Derry Courthouse, possibly the most bombed building in Ireland

Two Cathedrals dominate Derry's skyline more than 400 years after St Columb's (foreground) was built

Workers leaving the three-storey City Factory at the corner of Queen Street and Patrick Street, in the early 20th century

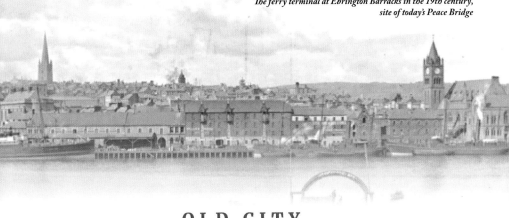

OLD CITY

The Plantation of Ireland in the 16th and 17th centuries led to dramatic changes in Derry's landscape.

Initial efforts to superimpose a new English city over the existing Irish mediaeval town, which sat on top of the 'Island of Derry', were thwarted by the native citizens, who burnt down the new experiment and killed the governor, George Paulet, in 1608.

Subsequently, the Livery Companies, which had been forcibly dispatched by 'money-hungry' King James I from London to colonise the region, surrounded their next attempt with massive schist walls, built 1613-1619 - a little over a mile in circumference - and it worked. Derry is now the only fully walled city of the era remaining in Europe.

Original plans for 500 houses within the walled city were reduced to 300, with 265 eventually being built on a grid system, centred on a town square (the Diamond) where a Civic Hall was later situated, before being replaced with the WWI Memorial standing today.

Four gates were originally installed, one on each flank of the walls - Bishop's Gate, Butcher Gate, Shipquay Gate and Ferryquay Gate - with Castle Gate, New Gate and Magazine Gate being added between 1790 and 1888.

(Today, you can find information points as you walk on the ramparts above these gates - and at other key points along the walls.)

The first Anglican cathedral built since the Reformation, St Columb's Cathedral was consecrated in 1633, inside the walls close to the site of An Teampaill Mór (The Big Church), which had been destroyed during Plantation. The Gothic cathedral would become of key strategic importance during subsequent sieges of Derry, including the Great Siege of 1689-90, when the city successfully defended itself against the Catholic King James II during the Williamite Wars.

In the late 18th century, the cathedral's spire was commissioned by Frederick Hervey (1730-1803), 'the edifying Bishop', who also built the first bridge across the River Foyle and the Mussenden Temple at Downhill. Today, the cathedral's chapter house contains Hervey's desk and artefacts from the sieges, including the locks from the city's gates.

Within 100 yards of the cathedral is the three-storey St Columb's Deanery (1833), which replaced the original deanery built on London Street in 1720, where the philosopher George Berkeley stayed while Dean of Derry. It also welcomed visitors such as Jonathan Swift, who once applied to become city dean - a very lucrative posting - but was turned down.

Just up the hill from the Deanery is Bishop St Courthouse (1817). Built from sandstone and described as 'Derry's finest Georgian building', it is possbily one of the city's most bombed edifices. Just on the other side of Bishop's Gate is the last remaining tower from the notorious Derry Gaol (1824), site of a mass jailbreak in 1943.

Along the walls close to Bishop's Gate, at the site of the former First Derry School (1894) is the Verbal Arts Centre, which features a priceless representation of the Táin Bó Cúailgne by Louis le Brocquy on its marble floor. The 17th century Derry playwright, George Farquhar, is commemorated with a plaque on the wall outside.

Heading down Grand Parade is the former garden (now carpark) of the Bishop's Palace, first built in 1753 and imaginatively remodelled by Hervey in 1800. The hymn-writer Cecil Frances Alexander, who lived in the palace with her husband William, (bishop 1867-96), is said to have been inspired by the view to pen 'There is a Green Hill Far Away'.

Adjacent on Grand Parade, and possibly the oldest continuously-inhabited site within the walls, is St Augustine's Church (1872), which most historians suggest is where Columban monks built their first monastery in the 6th Century. After the development of the main Augustinian monastery in the 12th century (An Teampall Mór), the 'little abbey' became known as the Dubh Regles (Black Church). In the early 17th century, it was recommissioned by the first English settlers and renamed the Church of God.

Upon exiting St Augustine's, the massive plinth looking out from the walls at Royal Bastion is the former home of the 81-foot Walker's Pillar (1826), erected in memory of Governor George Walker, who led the Williamite city during the Great Siege (1689-90), and which was blown up by the IRA in 1973.

The retrieved Walker statue still stands nearby, in the garden next to the Apprentice Boys Memorial Hall (1877) and new Siege Museum, which includes a full-scale model of how the city would have looked in the 17th century.

Heading down the walls towards Butcher Gate is found the First Presbyterian Church (1780) and the Blue Coat School Visitor Centre, which tells the story of presbyterianism in northwest Ireland and examines the age-old links between Ulster and Scotland.

During the late-19th and 20th century, Derry's main industry was shirt-making, and many of the old factories have been repurposed into tech businesses or in the case of the Nerve Centre on Magazine Street, a multi-media cultural hub.

At the Diamond stands the five-storey Austin's building (1830), until recently home to the oldest department store in the world.

Meanwhile, down the hill close to Shipquay Gate (which actually used to open onto the port prior to land reclamation, hence its name) is found the River Inn (1684), the city's oldest sited bar.

Just outside Shipquay Gate is the Guildhall (1890), home to Derry's civic parliament. One of the city's most iconic buildings, its clock tower was modelled on London's Big Ben. Rebuilt in 1908 after a fire, the Guildhall was targeted repeatedly as a centre of unionist power during the civil rights campaigns and early Troubles, but it later became a place of reconciliation, hosting both the Field Day cultural revival and later the Bloody Sunday Inquiry.

John Hume's peace awards - the Martin Luther King Prize, the Gandhi Prize and the Nobel Prize - are now on permanent display outside the building's Great Hall.

Close to the café at Guildhall's riverfront entrance [the main entrance opens onto Guildhall Square, site of three US presidential visits] are found the Harbour Museum (1882) and Custom House (1876).

Around the corner on Strand Road, outside Faller's Jewellers, hangs the Golden Teapot - a Derry landmark first displayed at Waterloo Place in

Shipquay Gate leading up to the old Town Hall, 18th century

1866. Fashioned from copper and reinforced with fibreglass, the only other one in the world is in Boston, where it commemorates the Boston Tea Party. (Derry's is ten years older!)

Artillery Street, at the heart of Derry's modern-day cultural quarter, houses the city's former Talbot Theatre (1795), which is now a diocesan office for the Church of Ireland. The adjacent New Gate was built, in part, to service theatre audiences, providing them with an easier route to the ferries on the river.

At Newmarket Street, just outside the walls lies St Columb's Hall (1886), the city's famous conference and entertainment venue, which has hosted luminaries such as Emmeline Pankhurst, Jim Reeves and Chubby Checker. It also encompasses a smaller 100-seat minor hall, later renamed the Little Theatre, which was one of the city's few dedicated arts venues during the Troubles.

Beyond the town-centre, there are also many vestiges of the old city worthy of viewing.

Work began on the neo-Gothic St Eugene's (Catholic) Cathedral on

Creggan Street in the 1840s and it was officially opened in 1873, with the spire being completed by 1903. It was the first cathedral built in the region after the Catholic Emancipation Act (1829), which marked an end to the Penal Laws.

A few hundred yards along Northland Road towards the city boundary is the Magee University Campus (1865), home today to around 3000 students, which housed a secret underground North Atlantic Command base during WWII. Derry has been campaigning for its own independent university of 10000 students for more than 60 years, a move repeatedly blocked by Stormont. Though new plans by the Royal Irish Academy, if adopted, could see numbers grow rapidly.

Across the Peace Bridge, in a 70-acre park close to the new Foyle Arena leisure centre, is found the recently-renovated St Columb's Park House and garden (1788). And also in the Waterside, on Glendermott Road, is the Derry Workhouse (1839), built to tackle poverty relief, which is open to the public on Heritage Days.

NEW CITY

During the early 20th century, Derry's main industry was shirt-making, with up to 10000 people (mostly women) employed by more than 40 factories.

Today, many of the old factories have been repurposed into tech businesses or in the case of the Nerve Centre (at the old Hunter's Factory on Magazine Street), a multi-media cultural hub.

Sited at the western end of Craigavon Bridge was the biggest of the former factories, Tillie & Henderson (1856) - at one time the largest shirt factory in the world. The iconic building was knocked down in 2003 after a series of mysterious fires, and the site will shortly feature a new apartment complex.

The former Rosemount Factory (1904), opposite the upper gates of Brooke Park, now housing a cluster of social enterprises, features on its roof a giant tribute to the city's shirt factories - an illuminated sign reading 'A Stitch in Time'.

During the 1950s and 60s, the city's biggest employer with more than 1200 staff was the BSR (Birmingham Sound Reproducers) plant at Bligh's Lane, which made record-players and tape-recorders. After its closure, the site hosted the Essex car-components factory, briefly a British army encampment, and then the United Technologies plant, before it was transferred to community ownership via Creggan Enterprises. Today, the Ráth Mór Social Enterprise Park features more than 60 businesses, from a medical centre to a supermarket, and employs 300 people.

At the Eastway entrance to the park is the Pat Mulkeen Garden, used frequently for outdoor events and concerts - where a 30-foot sculpture of a record turntable (by artist Locky Morris) and a tree planted by Labour leader Jeremy Corbyn mark the site's history.

Another brownfield site recently renovated is the city's old gasworks in the Bogside, which is today the Gasyard Centre community hub and cultural centre, and which will also feature the soon-to-be opened Peace Process Museum.

Former military sites are also being repurposed across the city, slowly turning swords into ploughshares. The former barracks at Ebrington, once home to the poet soldier Francis Ledwidge, is becoming a second city centre. Equipped with a massive outdoor concert venue, offices, shops, a gallery which hosted the Turner Prize, restaurants and, soon, a new hotel, Ebrington also features the Mute Meadow art installation.

The European Union-funded Peace Bridge (for pedestrians) linking Ebrington to the Guildhall was opened in 2011 in the run up to Derry's City of Culture Year (2013) and is now one of the city's best-known landmarks.

Also on the riverbank, about a mile downstream and on the other bank from Ebrington, is the former Fort George barracks, which also came back into public ownership in the early 2000s. A new science/tech centre (Catalyst) has already opened there, and plans have been mooted to develop a maritime and emigration museum at the old port, which is where tens of thousands of Irish people left the country for America, Australia and Britain during centuries past. Also here along the quayside, close to Sainsbury's, can be found Eamon O'Doherty's poignant sculpture The Emigrants.

In Creggan, the former British army base at Piggery Ridge is currently being transformed into a massive sporting complex for Sean Dolan's GAC. Meanwhile the former base at Clooney has been redeveloped into a pristine new school by Foyle College.

Other permanent monuments to our post-conflict society include the Foyle Street Peace Garden featuring the Peace Flame (2013) and Maurice

Harron's Hands Across the Divide statue (1992) at Craigavon Bridge.

Three new bridges have opened across the Foyle in the past 90 years. The Craigavon Bridge - the only double decker traffic bridge on these islands - opened in 1933. It replaced the Carlisle Bridge (1865), which superseded the river's first Earl Hervey Bridge (1790), a wooden cantilever bridge built in Boston MA and shipped across the Atlantic. The Foyle Bridge opened in 1984, becoming Ireland's longest suspension bridge. And the Peace Bridge opened in 2011.

While presidents, prime ministers and royalty from all over the world have made the trip to Derry, possibly our most celebrated visitor ever was Amelia Earhart who touched down just outside the city to complete her first solo transatlantic flight in May 1932. A plaque commemorating her feat was unveiled outside the Northern Counties building in 2019. Various streets and facilities in the city are also named in her honour, as is the lounge at City of Derry Airport, and a small museum at Ballyarnett close to the site of her descent, which operated for several years.

The recent conflict is represented in many forms across the city, most notably in the Bogside, home of Free Derry Corner, possibly Derry's most famous landmark. The corner marked the entry-point to Free Derry, a large area of Creggan, the Bogside and Brandywell, which was self-governed by local residents refusing entry to British personnel during the early Troubles. The iconic wall has been a rallying point for campaigners on many issues ever since.

Off Rossville Street at Joseph Place is found the Bloody Sunday Monument, erected in memory of the 14 civil rights marchers shot dead by British army

The Deanery on Bishop Street including the plaque commemorating the philosopher and former Dean of Derry, George Berkeley

Amelia Earhart lands in Derry in May 1932

paratroopers in the area on January 30, 1972. Close by, at the junction of Fahan Street is the H Block Monument, commemorating the ten hunger strikers (two of whom, Patsy O'Hara and Mickey Devine, were from Derry) who died in Long Kesh in 1981.

The award-winning Museum of Free Derry, located at Glenfada Park, site of several Bloody Sunday killings, focuses on the civil rights era and early Troubles.

The Rossville Street area also hosts a dozen gable wall murals, known as the People's Gallery, commemorating different aspects of the conflict. Themes represented include Civil Rights, Operation Motorman, Free Derry, Bloody Sunday, the Death of

Innocence, and the New Peace. Other murals in the Bogside include tributes to the Hunger Strikers, Republican women, and the revolutionary Ché Guevara, who had Irish ancestry.

Loyalist murals marking Protestant and Unionist heritage, including paintings of King William of Orange and the Siege of Derry, are found in the Fountain and at Bond Street in the Waterside.

Over the past decade, a series of new future-focused murals - including tributes to local heroes John Hume and Richard Moore - has been installed across the city by groups such as UV Arts. The most famous of these is undoubtedly the Derry Girls Mural on Orchard Street. The old Factory Wall on Eastway has also been reimagined as an open air gallery featuring a dozen new murals created by local schools in tandem with Creggan Enterprises.

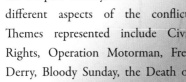

The Rosemount Factory with its sign celebrating the city's shirt-making heritage

BEACHES, PARKS & WOODLAND

BEACHES

Derry is a port town on the Foyle, a major river just a step away from the coast. You will find about a dozen first-class beaches within ten miles of the city - and another dozen within 20 or 30 miles.

For generations, the locals' favourite seaside spot has been Fahan, County Donegal - so much so that there used to be a railway terminal there. Fahan lies on Lough Swilly, just six miles from the city limits. Today, besides a stony beach and a massive sandy beach, the resort hosts a marina and a number of first-class restaurants. Fahan is also home to the Mura Cross, a carved Christian cross-slab dating back to the 7th century AD, which marks the grave of St Mura, who had been appointed abbot of the local monastery by St Colmcille.

Bordering Fahan is the Blue Flag beach of Lisfannon, with its magnificent views of Inch, Rathmullan and the Lough Swilly shoreline. Situated in a Natural Heritage area, it is an important home for many species of water birds. Lifeguards service this area from June to September. It also features toilets and a carpark.

The coastline itself has a rich history. In 1748, a 'foul-mouthed slave trader' called John Newton was rescued from a shipwreck in the Swilly during a storm. He was so moved by the experience he devoted the rest of his life to christianity and penned the hymn Amazing Grace - and the area is now referred to as Amazing Grace Country.

The former city reservoir, now home to Creggan Country Park

Fahan Beach

21

Lisfannon beach in 'Amazing Grace Country'

The beach at Lenan, County Donegal.

Lough Swilly (from the Irish Loch Súilí - the Lake of Shadows) was also the site of another famous shipwreck. In 1917 the SS Laurentic, carrying 3211 gold bars to Canada to pay for munitions, sank after hitting a mine, with the loss of more than 300 lives. Virtually all of the gold has been recovered, but several bars are still missing...

Less than two miles from Lisfannon, between North West Golf Club and Buncrana Golf Club, is Ludden beach. Ludden, which is almost two miles long, is very popular with sea-swimmers and families as it's well-sheltered.

Across the bay from Fahan on Inch Island are two beautiful beaches. At Inch Cove you can enjoy fishing from the pier, or paddleboarding and swimming from the little beach. And while car-parking can sometimes be tight in the high season, it's not too difficult to cycle from Derry. Inch Strand, also known as Mill Bay on the other side of the island, is more roomy if a little stonier.

Inch is also home to some very beautiful - and rare - birds in its Wildfowl Reserve Park, including wintering greylag geese, whooper swans, sandwich terns, black-head

gulls, herons and many more. The wildlife can be viewed from any of the many hides built along the 8km looped walk.

Buncrana Harbour features a beautiful beach and ferry port, which hosts cross-the-lough excursions to Rathmullan beach during the summer. Outside the town, there is a coastal walk along the shorefront, passing Fr Hegarty's Rock, and featuring beaches and swimming points at Ladies Bay, Neds Point, Strag(h)ill and Porthaw. (All also accessible by road.)

Further north on the Inishowen coastline, as it hits the open Atlantic, you will find Tullagh Strand, Pollan Strand, Ballyliffin beach, Lenan beach, the Five Finger(s) Strand, Culdaff beach and Kinnagoe Bay. The 'Tides Near Me' app will help you get the best times for swimming.

Along Lough Foyle's west bank, there are majestic beaches at Moville (plus a magnificent shore walk) and Stroove (with its beautiful lighthouse). Meanwhile on the east bank there are beaches at Benone, Downhill (with its legendary Vespan temple) and Castlerock. The coastal train journey from Derry to Castlerock takes about 30 minutes and is rated as one of the most beautiful rail trips in the world.

NI's highest waterfall in Ness Woods

Halloween Swim at Culdaff

Brooke Park in Winter

WOODS & PARKLAND

St Columb's Park in the Waterside is a 70-acre site, featuring, inter alia, a beautiful riverside walk/cycle, the ruins of a mediaeval church, an 18th century manor house and garden, as well as many modern amenities such as a leisure centre, children's playpark, cafés and sports pitches. (It also houses a significant percentage of the city's remaining red squirrel population.)

The 100-acre Creggan Country Park is host to three freshwater lakes, woodland, hedgerow, wildflower meadows and an activity centre with café-restaurant. Very popular with anglers, swimmers, canoeists and walkers.

Brooke Park, sandwiched in the city centre between the old Rosemount Factory and St Eugene's Cathedral, has had a much-needed makeover in recent years (led by the late Áine Downey among others). It now features a splendid café-restaurant affording views of the park, a sports centre with 4G and grass pitches, a judo and boxing complex, a bowling green, a market garden, rose gardens, and an ornamental fish pond.

Culmore Country Park opened to the public in 2016, marking the end of a £7 million project to restore a former landfill site. With magnificent views over the adjacent river Foyle, it features both woodland and grassland habitats.

Situated close to Amelia Earhart's landing spot, Ballyarnett Country Park extends over two acres of lakes and wetland is home to minks, otters, wild ducks and badgers. It also features a children's fun park.

Bay Road Nature Reserve is a 50-acre site on the banks of the Foyle, including woodland, grassland, salt marshes and mudflats. Opened in 2009, it features a wide range of wading and wintering birds.

Derry's oldest natural habitat is probably Prehen Woods, an ancient 20-acre woodland with majestic views over the city and the river. In spring, it is enveloped with 'carpets' of bluebells, celandine and wood anemone. It is also home to wildlife such as red squirrels,

foxes, hedgehogs, long-eared owls, sparrowhawks and butterflies. Watch out also for wooden sculptures created by Michael Rodgers, as you enjoy your walk.

About five miles outside the city, in the Faughan Valley, lies a cluster of woodlands, designated a Site of Special Scientific Interest (SSSI). These include Ness and Ervey Country Park & National Forest), featuring the highest waterfall in Ulster, (with visitor centre, toilets etc), Burntollet Wood, Brackfield Wood, Red Brae Wood, Killaloo Wood, Oaks Wood and Brackfield Bawn.

Ness's spectacular waterfall recently featured as one of the most romantic destinations in Ireland and Britain; legend has it that in the 18th century a young Romeo leapt across the falls in a death-defying attempt to escape his Juliet's father.

Hervey's Mussenden Temple at Downhill

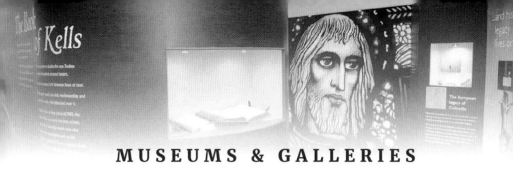

MUSEUMS & GALLERIES

Just inside Magazine Gate on the site of the ancient O'Doherty Fort, Derry's award-winning Tower Museum provides a comprehensive overview of the city's history from the prehistoric to the present.

Featuring countless collections, from politics to music to the Spanish Armada ships wrecked off the Donegal coast, starting in summer 2023 the museum will also house a Derry Girls exhibition, including props from the TV show such as school uniforms, Erin's diary and the girls' voting cards for the Good Friday Agreement referendum.

At Glenfada Park in the heart of the Bogside, the recently-extended Museum of Free Derry, focusing on the city's civil rights era, is one of the city's consistently most popular tourist destinations. Featuring exhibitions on the Battle of the Bogside, Internment, Bloody Sunday and Operation Motorman, the museum was developed in a block of flats outside which several men were killed and wounded on January 30, 1972. A new Museum of the Peace Process, which will focus on the work of Martin McGuinness, John Hume and Mitchel McLaughlin in resolving the conflict here, will be opening soon at the Gasyard Centre.

The three-storey Siege Museum on Society Street houses a permanent exhibition on the siege of 1689, described as one of the landmark events in British and Irish history, during which up to 30000 Protestant people held the walled city in the face of the Catholic king James II. The education and interactive experience also includes a display on the Associated Clubs of the Apprentice Boys of Derry.

The Harbour Museum on Harbour Square focuses on the North West's maritime heritage, and is being incorporated into a new facility currently being developed across the peace bridge at Ebrington.

In the grounds of the Long Tower church, in an old school dating back to 1813, is found Áras Cholmcille - St Columba Heritage Centre. Fitted with interactive and audio-visual displays, it is an ideal place to get an overview of the stories of Colmcille.

The recently-restored Foyle Valley Railway Museum, featuring a new clocktower, is based at a former train station beside Craigavon Bridge. It is run by Destined, a group for adults with learning disabilities, who serve as guides to the exhibits, rolling stock and artefacts.

The Void at Waterloo Place is a contemporary art gallery, with an international reputation and connections with a number of Turner Prize winners, that commissions and produces an extensive visual arts programme.

The Centre for Contemporary Art, CCA, on Artillery Street hosts an ambitious programme of contemporary art, focusing on emerging artists from Northern Ireland. CCA was one of the finalists for the Art Fund Museum of the Year in 2021, the world's largest museum prize, for its work supporting artists and audiences over the pandemic.

The Warehouse Gallery and retail outlet on Guildhall Street curates contemporary original pieces from talented artists from Ireland and beyond. Meanwhile the Cowley Cooper Fine Art Gallery and the Shipquay (formerly McGilloway) Gallery, both on Shipquay Street, showcase paintings and sculpture from Irish artists which are available for purchase.

Established in 1984, the award-winning Cultúrlann Ui Chanáin on Great James Street is now one of the most dynamic and innovative Irish language facilities anywhere on the island. Bunaithe i 1984, tá Cultúrlann Ui Chanáin ar Shráid Shéamais Mhór ar cheann de na háiseanna Gaeilge is dinimiciúla agus is nuálaí ar an oileán.

Within a short drive of Derry can be found several other museums and galleries of note, including: the Seamus Heaney HomePlace in Bellaghy, dedicated to the life and work of the Nobel Prize-winning poet; the Ulster American Folk Park outside Omagh, which tells the story of three centuries of Irish emigration in 30 exhibition buildings; and the Inishowen Maritime Museum & Planetarium in Greencastle.

TOURS & WALKS

The Visit Derry (visitderry.com) building on Waterloo Place is the North West's premier, all-encompassing tourist information centre.

Details of all tours, bespoke tours, tourism services and other visitor information can be found here. Visit Derry also offers official visitor passes, allowing access to ten attractions for discounted rates.

McNamara Tours offer walking and bus tours around the historic city, with focuses on the City Walls, the Guildhall, St Columb's Cathedral, the Tower Museum and the Railway Museum. The interactive tours last

around an hour and depart from the Guildhall.

Offering tours in English, French, Irish and other languages on request, Derry Blue Badge Tours cover all major subjects of interest including Irish history, politics, murals, the Troubles and the peace process, genealogy, emigration, music, sport and Christian heritage. Tours for schools are a speciality.

Martin McCrossan Derry City Walking Tours, operating from Carlisle Road, offer: a half-mile walk around the city walls with a comprehensive history of the city; a Derry Girls tour; a Spooky Derry tour (at Halloween); private bespoke tours; educational tours; and food tours.

Derrie Danders (dander is the favoured Derry word for stroll) offer mainstream cityside and Waterside walks. They also host bespoke tours on Influential Women of the North West; a Legenderry Musical Mystery Tour featuring Phil Coulter, Dana, Peter Cunnah, The Undertones, Josef Locke, Percy French Willie Loughlin and many more; and Blue Plaque tours of the Maiden City. In addition, they provide audio tours.

Tours of Derry, based at Great James Street, provide exclusive group tours of Derry and other areas of the North and North West, including a Game of Thrones tour.

LegenDerry Tours, on Foyle Street, offer city tours in English, French, Spanish, Italian and Catalan. Derry

Guided Tours offer political and history tours of the city.

Spirit of Derry tours offer a night of story and song for group parties at local hotels and venues.

Derry's massive graveyard now has its own tour, exploring headstones, history and funeral tradition. Friends of Derry City Cemeteries offer several daily tours from 11am to 6pm.

The explosion in Derry's food tourism sector has led to the establishment of a number of food/drink tours, including: the Foodie City Cycle around the Waterside and Cityside; the Derry Girls Food Tour (starts June 25); and beer masterclasses at the Walled City Brewery and the Northbound Brewery.

Derry Girls tours of the city are now very popular

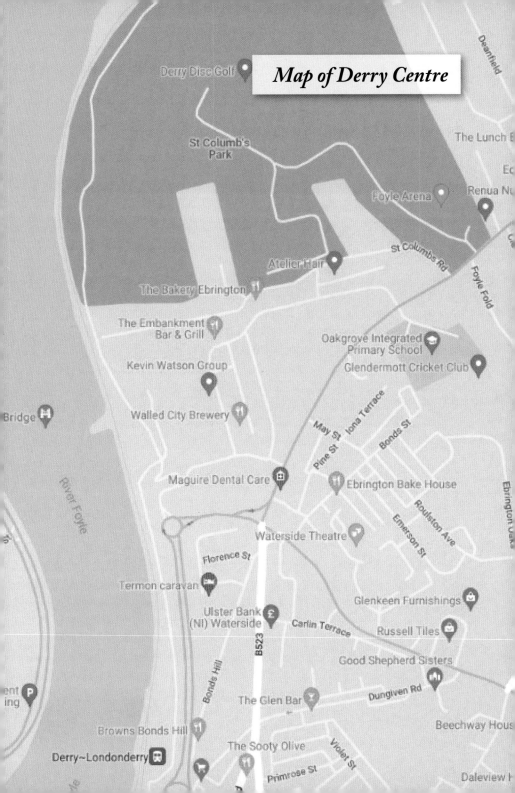

*St Columb's Hall,
which has hosted
names such as
Roy Orbison and
Emmeline Pankhurst*

MUSIC, CULTURE & SPORT

MUSIC IN THE DERRY AIR

**Derry is a global centre of music.
From Danny Boy to All Things Bright
and Beautiful, and from Teenage
Kicks to The Shape of You, music
across the world has been shaped
by singers and songwriters from
northwest Ireland for centuries.**

The region boasts Eurovision
winners, Ivor Novello winners,
Grammy winners and nominees,
award-winning choirs and big bands,
and chart-topping performers,
producers and writers.

During the city's many festivals,
virtually every hotel, restaurant, bar,
café, theatre, church, and other venue
hosts musical events, from orchestras
to soloists.

There just isn't enough space here to
list every live venue in the region - not
even the definitive 300-page Guildhall
Press history City of Music: Derry's
Music Heritage can provide that. But
if you follow your ears, here are a few
places you might end up...

Any time of the year, any day of the
week, you are almost certain to find
quality live acts in one of Waterloo
Street's many music bars. (Note the
use of 'quality' here. Derry doesn't
do second-class music; it's only when
people move out of the city that they
discover the rest of the world can't sing
like they do!) Check them all out and,
at the lower end of the street, be sure
and put your head into The Gweedore/
Peadar O'Donnell's, which for 50 years
has hosted top Irish and contemporary
music from international names like
Christy Moore and Peter Cunnah to
local heroes like Declan McLaughlin.

The list of other music establishments in the city centre is endless - changing and improving all the time thanks to the influx of new young talent such as Gemma Bradley, Reevah, Roe and Soak.

Sandinos Café Bar on Water Street has become a mecca for trad, rock, electronic, and world music. Bennigan's Bar & Jazz Club on John Street is another must visit.

On Magazine Street, Mason's, aka Brickwork Bar & Lounge, has been hosting live rock music since the early 1970s, including the legendary Toejam (fronted by the late, great Gerry Anderson) and The Undertones.

There's also an increasing number of venues catering for bigger bands, showbands and crowds. When you're in town be sure and check out the listings for all the hotels, and also Da Vinci's, the Corinthian Ballroom (City Hotel), the Dungloe, Silver Street, the Bentley, the Central Bar, the Metro, Link 48, the Taphouse and the Blackbird.

Several of the city's old churches also host music events. Always worth checking if St Augustine's on the Walls has anything planned.

For an all-round cultural experience, there are few better places to visit than the Nerve Centre, the award-winning multimedia arts complex on Magazine Street. Opened in 1999, it features a 700-capacity concert/performance venue, two arthouse cinemas [the Centre runs the annual Foyle Film Festival, the biggest in NI], a top restaurant, rehearsal and music-teaching space, a range of top digital suites for training in film, animation and music.

Set up by the North West Musicians' Collective in the 1980s, the Nerve Centre on Magazine Street is the number one multimedia arts complex in the North.

DRAMA & SCREEN

After a few decades of a lull during the Troubles, theatre-lovers are today spoilt for choice. The Millennium Forum, which opened on Newmarket Street in 2001, is a magnificent facility, complete with Ireland's biggest stage, a 1000-seater auditorium, several large minor halls, a gallery, a restaurant and a café. The Forum has a full, year-long programme, catering for all tastes, from

The Verbal Arts Centre on the Walls

touring West End dramas, to comedy, to opera, to Daniel O'Donnell (who films a TV show here for TG4) to Derry-connected Snow Patrol.

Just on the other side of East Wall from the Forum is St Columb's Hall, opened in 1888 and now Derry's longest-serving entertainment venue. Originally a Catholic temperance hall, in its time it has served as a theatre, cinema and opera house. And it has hosted revolutionary thinkers such as Emmeline Pankhurst, musicians such as Hank Williams and Roy Orbison, and, of course, the annual Derry Féis on Easter Week. Besides the main 900-seater hall, the massive complex also features a 100-seat Little Theatre (currently being refurbished), which was one of the very few arts venues to

remain open throughout the Troubles. (See *Derry at Play* by Gerry Downey for more.)

Just uphill on East Wall, at Artillery Street, is found The Playhouse. Established in 1992 at the site of a 19th century school, it houses a 175-seat theatre, a dance studio, a gallery and extensive education/outreach departments. It also features its own in-house drama companies, responsible for critically-acclaimed productions such as Hume Beyond Belief and Theatre of Witness.

Besides being the cornerstone for Derry's civil rights movement, The Guildhall has served for more than a century as a venue (750-plus capacity) for everything from Spider Kelly's championship boxing matches to Paul Robeson concerts, and from

Ebrington Square, which hosts major outdoor events (up to 10000) including concerts, such as the Beach Boys and the Radio One Big Weekend

the first base for the Field Day Theatre Company to the venue for the Bloody Sunday Inquiry.

With a capacity of 372, the Waterside Theatre is housed within a beautifully-converted old factory on Glendermott Road. With a year-long programme of arts, educational and cultural events, it also houses a full-screen cinema, a café and lounge bar, and free on-site parking.

Arts-loving visitors might also check out the schedule for the 270-capacity Alley Theatre in Strabane which is only 14 miles/25 minutes down the road.

The new Foyle Theatre, built on Strand Road as part of the North West Regional College's recent expansion, seats 150 people. And the Great Hall at Magee University, which hosts drama, music, book launches and exhibitions, has a capacity of 180.

The city's outdoor performance areas include Guildhall Square, (which hosted the march past for US marines heading for the D-Day landings), Ebrington Square and the Craft Village which is now part-roofed.

The two biggest cinema complexes in the North West are the Omniplex on Strand Road and Brunswick in Pennyburn, both of which have children's clubs. Within a 30 minutes drive, in Donegal you can find: St Mary's' Hall in Buncrana, which houses a beautiful old two-screen cinema; the eight-screen Century Cinema in Letterkenny, with backstage bar and grill; and the Eclipse Cinema in Lifford.

Guildhall Square which hosts major outdoor events, including live theatre, street markets and a number of Presidential visits.

SPORTS

Derry has a great history of sporting giants including Olympians Roisin Lynch, Aileen Morrison and Liam Ball, champion boxers Charlie Nash and the two Spider Kellys, international footballers John Crossan and James McClean, and many more.

Many of our household names learned their trades in primitive enough conditions. But today, thankfully there are many first-class sporting facilities in the North West where visitors can play, practice or spectate.

Derry's two biggest stadia both are situated along the Lone Moor Road, just a couple of hundred yards apart. Celtic Park, Derry GAA's County Ground, has a capacity of 18000 for Gaelic football and hurling games. The Ryan McBride Brandywell Stadium next door has been used as Derry City's home ground since the 1920s, with a break for over a decade during the early Troubles, after the Northern league refused to let the Candy Stripes host games at the ground. Thanks to a campaign led by former players Terry Harkin, Tony O'Doherty, Eddie

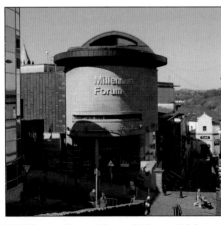

The Millennium Forum on Newmarket Street, which features the city's biggest auditorium

Mahon and Eamonn McLaughlin, in 1985 the club was welcomed into the Southern league. Both Celtic Park and the Brandywell regularly host community events and coaching sessions for youngsters when not being used for big games. The Brandywell also has an indoor sports centre open to the public.

If you want to stay in shape during your visit, there are many other sports centres and facilities in the city. The Foyle Arena in St Columb's Park, and the Templemore Sports Complex on Buncrana Road are the two biggest multi-purposes facilities, both featuring 25m pools, state-of-the-art gyms, indoor sports halls and a myriad outdoor pitches and tracks. The Arena, which is also a centre of excellence for judo and wrestling, features the biggest indoor climbing wall in the region.

Swimmers can also avail of the City Baths on William Street, the White Horse Hotel at Campsie, and the City Hotel on Queen's Quay, all of which also feature gyms. While open-water swimmers can take their pick from numerous beaches and lough-pools, all within a 30-minute drive of the city centre. (See Beaches)

The Bishops' Field Centre in Creggan hosts a wide range of indoor and outdoor facilities, including a championship-sized basketball court. The recently-renovated Brooke Park Sports Centre also features a bowling green, 4G pitches and a new contact sports centre for boxing and judo.

Other sporting facilities in the city include the Sean Dolan's GAA Complex in Creggan, the Leafair Well-Being Village and the Shared Village Complex in the Waterside.

The city is home to a growing number of running clubs, catering for all ages and abilities, and there is a weekly 5k Park Run on Saturday mornings from the riverside at Sainsbury's to St Columb's Park - all are welcome. For the serious trainers, there are numerous gyms and early-morning boot camps across the city, where the many hills can test even the most seasoned athletes.

Cycling has become a lot more popular since the development of the greenways (Foyle Valley, Waterside, Culmore/Muff, Strathfoyle, Inch Island) along the river and across the border. Details and maps of the greenways, North and South, can be found online.

Northwest Ireland is home to some of the finest and most picturesque golf courses in the world. On the outskirts of Derry, there are first-class courses at Ballyarnett (Foyle), and Prehen (City of Derry). Within a half-hour drive you can find the North West Golf Club at Lisfannon, the Buncrana Golf Club (9-hole), the Faughan Valley Golf Centre in Eglinton and Strabane Golf Club. Championship courses within 45 minutes of Derry include the Royal Portstewart and Ballyliffin.

Angling is a hugely popular recreation in the North West. The 100-acre Creggan Country Park operates a 'put and take' trout fishery, while also offering a large range of activities for the non-anglers in the family including walks, kayaking, swimming, pier-jumping and raft building. In the Waterside, there is the Oaks Fishery on Judges Road.

The Foyle (and its many tributaries such as the Faughan, Finn and Strule) has a reputation for excellent salmon and trout. Licensing - season tickets or day passes - is managed through the Loughs Agency and the Faughan Anglers Association.

EATING OUT:
DESTINATION DELICIOUS

This region has a massive culinary heritage.

At different times in its 1500-year-plus history, Derry has been a world trade centre for herring, salmon, whiskey and, even, (during WWII) rabbits. And Derry emigrants, according to Emmett McCourt's award-winning history Feast or Famine: A Cultural Food Journey of the North West, are responsible for the development of the first potato plantations (note, not yams) and apple orchards in North America.

Seafood, unsurprisingly, given our proximity to North Atlantic waters, is a local speciality, with Inishowen fish restaurants such as Kealy's in Greencastle and The Red Door at Fahan acclaimed all over the world.

Another 19th-century industry making a comeback is distilling. Watts Distillery, which closed in 1921 and is soon to be reopened on Foyle Street, produced Tyrconnell, the biggest-selling whiskey in North America pre-Prohibition. In the Waterside, The Quiet Man whiskey distillery opened recently on Rossdowney Road.

During the Troubles, dining out in Derry at night was for many years confined to hotels (of which there were very few) and a single steakhouse. However, over the past 30 years, the restaurant industry has flourished, so much so that the city was recently pronounced 'Destination Delicious' at the NI Food & Drink Awards.

All tastes are catered for, from the simple local fare to cordon bleu, including two Michelin-recommended restaurants, Artis in the Craft Village and Browns on Bonds Hill.

For what it's worth, the production team behind this handbook swear by Fiorentini's Café (fish, chips and home-made ice-cream) on Strand Road, The Old Docks Bar & Grill (steakhouse) on Queen's Quay and Yellow Button Café (for lunches) at Ráth Mór.

But rather than trying to play local favourites, we are instead including here the top 25 restaurants as recommended by TripAdvisor reviewers last year (with the assurance that there are as many more, and more again, just as good if not better).

Top Twenty-Five Derry Dinner Restaurants 2022 as recommended on TripAdvisor

1.Mekong (Asian street food)
dishcult.com/restaurant/mekong1
07835 330360

2. Cedar (Lebanese)
cedarlebanese.webs.com
028 7137 3868

3. Browns Bonds Hill
(fine dining)
brownsbondshill.com
028 7134 5180

4. Shipquay Hotel
(Irish, European)
shipquayhotel.com/restaurant
028 7126 7266

5. The Sooty Olive
(Irish, European)
dishcult.com/restaurant/
thesootyolive 028 7134 6040

6. Spaghetti Junction (Italian)
spaghettijunction.com
028 7141 4242

7. Mama Masala (Italian,
Indian) just-eat.co.uk/restaurants-
mamamasala-edenballymore/
menu 028 7126 6646

8. Fitzroys (Irish, European)
fitzroysrestaurant.com
028 7126 6211

Walled City Brewery (restaurant) on Ebrington Square

9. Timberquay (Irish, European)
timberquay.com
028 7137 0020

**10. Pyke 'N' Pommes
(restaurant and street food)**
pykenpommes.ie 028 716 72691

**11. Browns in Town
(Irish, European)**
brownsintown.com
028 7136 2889

**12. Quaywest (European,
British)** quaywestrestaurant.com
028 7137 0977

**13. Walled City Brewery
(European, contemporary)**
walledcitybrewery.com
028 7134 3336

**14. 2 North
(street food)**
028 7131 2313

**15. Badgers Bar and Restaurant
(Irish, bar)** 028 7136 3306

**16. The Exchange
(European, British)**
exchangerestaurant.com
028 7127 3990

Spaghetti Junction, an old-style Italian trattoria on William Street

17. Link 47 (European, live music) link47.co.uk
028 7187 4727

18. The Bentley (Irish, bar)
thebentleybar.com
028 7137 1665

19. El Tapas Grá (Spanish)
eltapasgra.com
028 7127 1801

20. Castle Street Social (Irish, international)
zmenu.com/castle-street-social-londonderry-uk-online-menu
028 7137 2888

21. The Gate Bistro (healthy, Irish)
thegatebistroandcocktailbar.com
07379 492261

22. Arbutus at the Forum (European, Central European)
028 7137 2492

23. The Belfray (grill, bar)
028 7130 1480

24. Guapo (Mexican, fast food)
028 7136 5585

25. Saffron (Indian, Asian)
028 7126 0532

1. *Thatched Cottage Café and Gallery
in the Craft Village*
2. *The Old Dock's Bar & Grill
on Queen's Quay*
3. *Coupé Restaurant on Shipquay Street*

Young people from all of the world take part in Derry's Halloween Carnival week

FUN FOR CHILDREN

From aquariums to ziplining, northwest Ireland is a paradise for children from the sedate to the very active. Besides all the beaches, riverfront attractions and sports facilities already outlined, there are literally dozens of other child-specific amenities, programmes and courses to keep the younger members of the family more than entertained while you are here.

Young soccer lovers, who despair of the summer break, take heart! Derry is the place to be in July, when the annual O'Neill's Foyle Cup tournament sees more than 500 teams from all over the world take part in the biggest youth soccer event on the island. (This year's competition from July 17-22, caters for boys, girls, ladies, and athletes with disabilities.) There are also weeklong soccer camps at grounds across the city, throughout the summer - booking is advised.

Gaelic football and hurling training schools, aka Cúl (goal) Camps, are also run throughout the summer months at different GAA clubs across the region. The weeklong camps for both boys and girls can be booked online.

Summer swimming courses for learners or intermediates, and life-saving courses for advanced swimmers, are available at the Foyle Arena and Templemore Sports complex and can be booked through the Derry/ Strabane Council website. Lessons are also available at the region's private pools. Sea swimming is very popular in the North West at a selection of Blue Flag beaches, some of which also host regular fun days, with sea-slides etc.

Swimmers, canoeists, kayakers and young anglers should also check out Creggan Country Park, which offers an extensive all-year-round programme of activities. The facility also features some beautiful walks, a café restaurant and shop.

For lovers of the great outdoors, Far and Wild, based at St Columb's Park, offers a wide-range of adventurous activities including rock climbing, paddleboarding, kayaking, biking, rollerblading and boomboarding. And if you like speed, there are karting tracks at the Halfway (Burnfoot) and Castlefin.

Oakfire Adventures on the Glenshane Road offer adventure courses and ziplining through some of the most picturesque forest land in Ireland. It also hosts the Oakfire Paintballing Course (over 16s).

LockNLoad, which has indoor facilities in Springtown and outdoor ones at Creggan Country Park, hosts Airsoft (ages 12+), Reball (low impact paintball 9+), laser tag (7+), nerf wars (6+) and archery tag (10+).

Children who enjoy animals and wildlife will be spoilt for choice in the North West. Barrontop Farm in Donemana features everything from ducks to ostriches, and also a café and soft play area for the younger children. Lurgyback Farm at Letterkenny is centuries old, with all sorts of friendly farm animals and has a tea-room, snack area and play park.

Ducks, chickens, pigs and an aviary can also be found at the Sperrin Fun Farm, at Feeny, as can an indoor adventure park with bouncy castles for young children.

The Riverwatch Aquarium on the Foyle at Prehen captures the journey

The Playhouse on Artillery Street

The brown bear at Wild Ireland

of the river and the lough, and the wide variety of freshwater and marine life that inhabits it.

Wild Ireland at Burnfoot, a sanctuary for exploited and endangered animals, takes you back in time to an ancient Ireland inhabited by bears, wolves, lynx and wild boar. It takes about two hours to see everything, and has a tea-room, shop and picnic area.

Equestrian enthusiasts can avail themselves of lessons and/or treks from a number of stables across the North West, including Lenamore, Claudy, City of Derry, Faughanvale and Ardmore.

There are many purpose-built outdoor play facilities for youngsters across the North West, including at Brooke Park, St Columb's Park, Irish Street, the Brandywell, Bull Park, Redcastle, Moville, Buncrana seafront and the Pennyburn PlayTrail.

Boot camps (EBA Camps) and multi-skilled camps, offering everything from boxercise to walking football (Danderball,) are available for most age groups from the Council's leisure centres. The Foyle Arena also organises a week-long Junior Climbing Camp during the summer.

The Magazine Studios

If you like your fun indoors, the Brunswick Moviebowl in Pennyburn is the North West's biggest entertainment complex, complete with 7-screen cinema kids clubs, 16-lane bowling alley, a pool hall, games arcade, jungle gym, café and a licensed restaurant. The Arena 7 Moviebowl in Letterkenny (less than 30 minutes away) features similar amenities plus a laser quest facility. Under-12s can also enjoy an indoor adventure park at Wains World in Buncrana. The Bounce Away indoor party venue at Maydown now also organises special sessions for autistic children.

Summer camps in speech & drama, art, singing, music and cooking for children between four and 12 are available at the Playhouse (Artillery Street) during the summer. It also hosts weekly classes in ballet, Irish dancing, and yoga for four to 11-year-olds.

The Nerve Centre, on Magazine Street, offers a range of summer courses in creative media, including photography, electronic music, coding and 3D modelling. The centre also hosts a Music Hothouse for young people between 11-18, in which musicians can develop their songwriting talents, form a band, and receive mentoring and one-to-one support. And young filmmakers (16-19) can avail of a new course in VFX, instructing them in how to produce digital visual effects for short films.

1. *Creggan Country Park offers a wide range of outdoor and water-based activities for young people.*
2. *O'Neill's Foyle Cup Parade through the city centre. The July soccer event features thousands of youth players (ages c.7–21) from all over the world.*
3. *Boom boarding at St Columb's Park with Far and Wild*

O'Neill's Foyle Cup

The Imbolc Festival at Cultúrlann Uí Chanáin

FESTIVALS

For decades now, Derry has been the 'world capital' of Halloween, with the autumn event attracting tens of thousands of visitors to the North West every year. But if you're not into dressing up and scaring your neighbours, don't worry, the region's cultural calendar has got something that caters for everyone's taste.

Always a party-loving people, Derry's designation as the first City of Culture in 2013 forced the populace to up their game, with hundreds of public sector staff (and many ordinary citizens besides) qualifying as World Tourism Hosts. This means that you never have far to go to meet someone who'll help you find whatever event you want to see, hear or participate in.

February 1st sees the official start of the Irish Spring (Teacht an Earraigh),

and this is marked each year with the Imbolc International Music Festival, run by the Derry Cultúrlann. The programme includes traditional Irish, folk, bluegrass and cutting-edge music across a wide variety of city-centre venues. Fringe activities include art exhibitions, sculpture, drawing and installation, photography and printmaking.

March sees the city hold its Spring Carnival, encompassing St Patrick's week. The main March 17 parade, from Bishop's Street to Council Offices, involves schools, youth groups and community associations and is second only to Halloween Carnival in terms of size and flamboyance. Surrounding events include Irish traditional sessions, food expos, and Irish dancing exhibitions.

Late March is also traditionally the time for the Strabane Spring Drama

Halloween fireworks

piano at Magee University.

Ireland's leading electronic music festival, Celtronic, takes place at assorted city centre venues in April and May, including the Nerve Centre, Echo Echo Dance Studios, Cultúrlann Uí Chanáin and Sandinos. The festival, which attracts the top names from all over Europe, operates a strict 'no phones on the dancefloor' policy.

Easter Week is traditionally the time for one of Derry's biggest festivals and competitions, Féis Dhoire Cholmcille which recently notched up its first century in business. A celebration of all the traditional Irish arts, including music, singing, recitation and dancing, it involves all age groups from the very young to seniors.

Festival at the Alley Theatre. The 10-day festival features troupes from all over Ireland.

March/April also sees the hosting of the Walled City Music Festival at various locations across the region, including Christchurch, off Northland Road. The festival includes the best in classical, contemporary and choral music. Later in the year, the WCMF organisation also hosts an international

Music legends from all over the world gather in the North West for the May Bank Holiday weekend and the City of Derry Jazz & Big Band Festival. Tens of thousands of spectators from home and away gather at more than 60 venues across the city, indoors and outdoors, including many

The biennial Maritime Festival takes place along the Foyle in early summer.

pop-up sessions. Virtually every big name on the jazz circuit has played the festival over the past 30 years from Van Morrison and John Coltrane to perennial favourites The Jive Aces.

June is a busy month for celebrations in Derry, with the Clipper Yacht Race and Maritime Festival tipped to return in 2024. For centuries the city has been marking the feast day of its founder, St Colmcille, on June 9, with a series of church and community events, including pilgrim walks and the blessing of the Columban Wells. The same month also sees the Every Voice Festival, hosted by Allegri, take place in Derry, Tyrone and Donegal, featuring vocal ensembles and choirs,

workshops, pop-up performances, flash mobs and community events.

Vintage car enthusiasts cruise to Ebrington Square in June/July for the four-day Celtic Car Classic Festival, which tours Ireland. In early July, the International Piano Festival takes place at Magee University.

July also sees the region's top local music festival take place at Limavady. The Stendhal Festival is a regular winner of best small festival and best family friendly festival awards.

In July 2023, the GAA World Games will take place at the Derry Centre of Excellence in Owenbeg, with upwards of 2000 players from all over the world doing battle in hurley, camogie, football and ladies football competitions.

In Donegal, meanwhile, the Earagail Arts Festival, founded in the 1980s, takes place over three weeks in July at venues across the north of the county from Letterkenny to Tory Island. The dozens of events include dance, music, theatre, masterclasses, street circuses, spoken word sessions, visual arts and film shows. In Glenties, in the south of the county, the MacGill Summer School in July has become Ireland's leading international thought forum for leaders to discuss critical issues facing the island, Europe and the world.

St Patrick's Day in Derry is second only to Halloween in size

The second week of August sees Derry host the Maiden City Festival, a diverse cross-cultural series of events commemorating the 1689 Siege. Events include street theatre, Scottish dancing, historical walks and talks and fireworks displays. The festival culminates in the Relief of Derry parade on the Saturday closest to August 12.

The Gasyard Féile in August is one of the biggest arts and cultural community festivals in the North West. Centred at the Gasyard but taking place in a wide range of city centre venues, the two-week programme features debate, politics, economics, song, theatre, film shows and much more.

A relatively new addition to the North West's cultural calendar is Dylanfest, which takes place in Moville towards the end of August. It is already widely described as the best Bob Dylan Festival in Ireland.

October sees the City of Derry International Choir Festival take place at venues including cathedrals, halls and concert theatres across the North West. The programme includes guests from all over the world, competitions, workshops and loads of live performances.

At the end of October, Derry's week-long (at least) Halloween festival has now acquired legendary status, with every corner of the city filled with activity from fire-eaters to ghost tours. It all culminates in the grand parade and firework display on Hallween night - a night not to be missed and worth a book in its own right.

In November, Northern Ireland's only Oscar and BAFTA-affiliated film festival, the Foyle Film Festival, takes place over ten days at various venues. Established in 1987 and led by the Nerve Centre, the festival features scores of screenings open to the public.

It has attracted many top names in its time, including Oscar-winning actors, directors and writers.

In December, Derry's Winterland Market (at Guildhall Square) and Craft Fair draw massive crowds of visitors, rounding off the year with good cheer while sourcing some great locally-produced goods and presents.

Please note - this is only a flavour of some of the bigger events that take place any given year. For the most up-to-date information, be sure and check with visitderry.com.

The annual Foyle Pride Parade takes place in August

The Austin's building – home of the oldest department store in the world – is shortly to become a hotel

RETAIL THERAPY

Value, quality, originality and accessibility are watchwords of retail in the North West. For decades, the region has demonstrated a particularly competitive edge, as both sides of the border vie for local custom.

Over the past fifty years, the prices of items such as electronic goods, fuel, tobacco and alcohol, and luxury goods, have fluctuated - sometimes wildly - North and South. (E.g., drink is currently cheaper in the North, while fuel is cheaper in the South.) So retailers know that if they are to compete along the border they have to give you their best offer up front, as they can't risk you hopping across to the other jurisdiction.

In Derry, you will find a wide range of retail outlets, from from the bespoke and bijou to the multinational chains.

Local specialities include food, whiskey, (sports) shirts and knitwear, crystal, wood and steel-wrought products, jewellery, pottery, candles, soaps, lotions, books and cards.

The city has several major shopping malls/areas: Foyleside, the Richmond Centre, Crescent Link, and Lisnagelvin Shopping Centre, Lisnagelvin Retail Park, Quayside, Faustina Retail Park, the Ráth Mór Centre and Northside Village Centre.

There are also dozens of shops along the city-centre streets, at Waterloo Place, in the Craft Village and on/off Spencer Road; and several major supermarkets such as Sainsbury's and Lidl.

Foyleside Mall is home to more than 50 outlets

Foyleside was the North's largest mall when it opened in the 1990s. Today, it hosts more than fifty national, multinational and local outlets, including: House of Fraser, Marks & Spencer, Boots, Next, Waterstones, Sports Direct, McDonald's, Dunne's Stores, Starbucks, a hairdressers, a barbers, and a food court.

Derry's oldest mall is the Richmond Centre on Shipquay Street/Ferryquay Street (1984). It has more than 35 retailers under the one roof, including some major High Street names. Outlets include: Nando's, Vodafone, Shoe Zone, The Bag Shop, Bonmarché, Jack & Jones, JD Sports, Trespass, and several cafés.

Situated between the Richmond Centre and Foyleside, on the site of the former Rialto Cinema on Newmarket Street, is Primark - featuring womens, mens, kids, beauty and home departments over three floors.

Crescent Link, in the Waterside, is Derry's largest 'out-of-town' mall (though it is less than a mile from the Foyle Bridge and within the city boundaries). It hosts a range of major

Foyle Books, as featured in the Derry Girls finale

Lisnagelvin Shopping Centre, which opens 6am until midnight, features 20 shops and kiosks, with a Tesco Superstore as its anchor. Its outlets include: C5 Clothing, Luxe, Toytown, Lloyds Pharmacy, Subway and The Sandwich Company. Immediately on the other side of the A6, Lisnagelvin Retail Park features several major outlets including Next, TK Maxx and Matalan.

chain stores including Homebase DIY, Currys, Next Home, Argos, Halfords and B&M, along with several cafés/fast food outlets, a gym, and two small supermarkets - Tesco Express and Marks & Spencer Simply Food.

Quayside on Strand Road is anchored by another Tesco Superstore. It also hosts a number of pharmacies and semi-chems, a barber's shop, a gift shop and a bargain store.

At the corner of the Strand Road and Buncrana Road, are a number of large outlet stores, including Harry Corry, Home Bargains and B&M. And on the outskirts of the city on Buncrana Road is the Faustina Retail Park, anchored by The Range and Dunelm.

The Richmond Centre hosts 35 retail stores

Ráth Mór on Blighs Lane, is a four-acre business park, anchored by Eurospar supermarket. It features 60 businesses and retail outlets; among which are: a pharmacy, a florist, a phone shop, a thrift store, and two barbers. Northside Village Centre, on Glengalliagh Road, features a supermarket, a card shop, thrift store, pharmacy, and a number of hair salons.

There are also numerous outlets across the North West for collectors of vintage products, (books, clothes, records and antiques). Little Acorns Bookstore on Great James Street and Foyle Books in the Craft Village (as featured in the Derry Girls finale) both are home to tens of thousands of new and previously-owned books. And the vintage marketplace Yellow Yard on Palace Street has a clothing section, a gift shop, a book outlet and a record shop.

If you fancy a short road-trip, half an hour away in County Donegal, you will find the Letterkenny Shopping Centre and the Letterkenny Retail Park. Letterkenny Shopping Centre has over 70 outlets including Dunnes Stores, Marks & Spencer, Next, River Island and H&M. Letterkenny Retail Park has 30 stores including Homebase, Argos, Currys PC World and Next Home. Fifteen minutes further out the road is found McElhinney's of Ballybofey, one of the largest department stores in Ireland outside Dublin. Strabane Retail Park, 15 miles from Derry, features 30 outlets including Homebase, Argos and Next Home.

The award-winning Little Acorns Bookstore on Gt James Street.

61

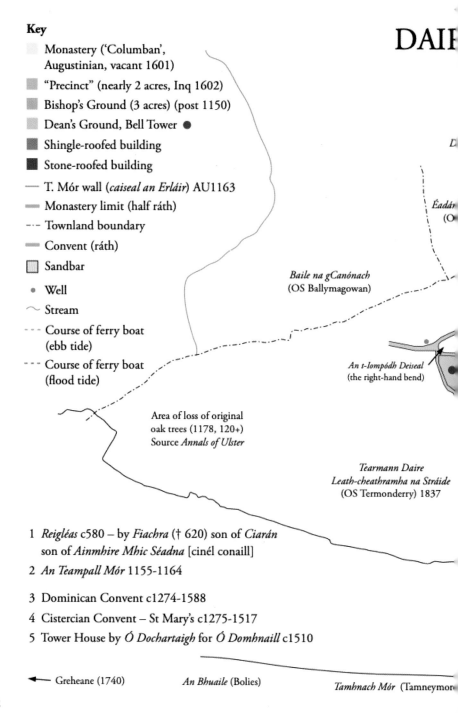

Key

Monastery ('Columban', Augustinian, vacant 1601)

"Precinct" (nearly 2 acres, Inq 1602)

Bishop's Ground (3 acres) (post 1150)

Dean's Ground, Bell Tower ●

Shingle-roofed building

Stone-roofed building

— T. Mór wall (*caiseal an Erláir*) AU1163

━ Monastery limit (half ráth)

--- Townland boundary

━ Convent (ráth)

▨ Sandbar

• Well

~ Stream

--- Course of ferry boat (ebb tide)

--- Course of ferry boat (flood tide)

DAI

D

Éadá
(O

Baile na gCanónach
(OS Ballymagowan)

An t-Iompódh Deiseal
(the right-hand bend)

Area of loss of original oak trees (1178, 120+)
Source *Annals of Ulster*

Tearmann Daire
Leath-cheathramha na Stráide
(OS Termonderry) 1837

1 *Reigléas* c580 – by *Fiachra* († 620) son of *Ciarán* son of *Ainmhire Mhic Séadna* [cinél conaill]

2 *An Teampall Mór* 1155-1164

3 Dominican Convent c1274-1588

4 Cistercian Convent – St Mary's c1275-1517

5 Tower House by *Ó Dochartaigh* for *Ó Domhnaill* c1510

◄— Greheane (1740) *An Bhuaile* (Bolies) *Tamhnach Mór* (Tamneymor